MELODY LINE • LYRICS • CHORDS

THE ROBERT EARL KEEN SONGBOOK

Front Cover Photo: © 1994 Peter D. Figen, All Rights Reserved

ISBN 978-0-7935-4431-8

HAL•LEONARD®
CORPORATION
7777 W. BLUEMOUND RD. P.O. BOX 13819 MILWAUKEE, WI 53213

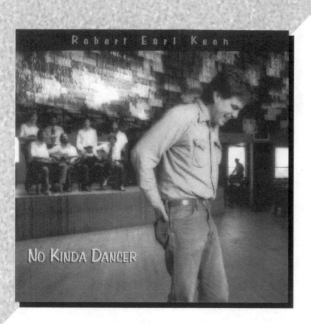

Robert Earl Keen
Calendar by Pat Johnson
Circa 1983

The house at 302 Church Street, College Station, Texas. Condemned during Robert's occupancy. However, he continued to live there with Sunny Fitzsimons and Bryan Duckworh until he graduated. The house was owned by Mr. Jack Boyett, the "seventy years of Texas" written about by Robert and fellow Aggie, Lyle Lovett.

Publicity
Photo
taken by
Jeff Kopp,
1981

The Armadillo Jackal

Words and Music by
ROBERT EARL KEEN

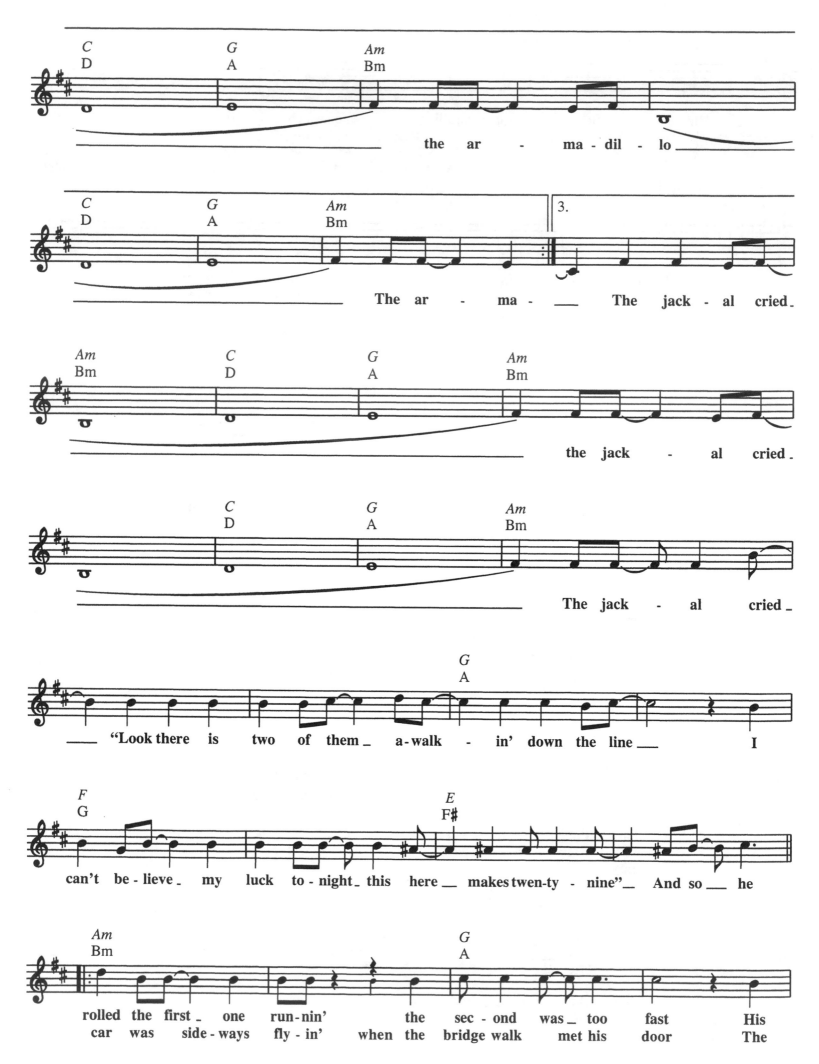

Swervin' In My Lane

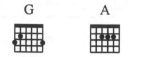

Words and Music by
ROBERT EARL KEEN

Swing (♩ = 125)

VERSE

Some-times I don't know ___ what I'm do - in'
day you drove a - way ___ I thought I'd nev - er
When and if I ev - er fi - n'ly pass ___ you

some-times all my days ___ are filled ___ with rain ___
could love an - oth - er How ___ else could ___ I feel ___
oh when I do and if ___ I'm still ___ a - live ___

___ As I trav - el down life's high -
___ But now when you run in -
___ I won't nev - er see ___

- way things ain't go - in' my ___ way 'cause there's ___ al -
- to me I can't be - lieve I could ___ not see you're ___ all ___
___ you 'cause I'm rip - in' out the rear ___ view and I'm ___ slip -

CHORUS
N.C.

- ways some - one swerv - in' in ___ my lane ___   You keep a - swerv - in' in my
__ tanked up ___ and no ___ one's at ___ the wheel_   You keep a - swerv - in' in my
- pin' it ___ on in - to o - ver - drive_   But you're still swerv - in' in my

lane   and it's caus-in' lots of dan - ger   I'm a-honk-in' on my
lane   and it's caus-in' lots of dan - ger   I'm a-cuss-in' out your
lane   and it's caus-in' lots of dan - ger   I'm a-stomp-in' on the

horn
name   I'm a-shoot-in' you the fin - ger   I keep a-switch-in' on my
foot feed

bright lights   but you're just too dim to know_____   When you're swerv-in' on life's

1., 2.

high - way   you're run-nin' some-one off the road   (2.) The
    (3.)

3.

road _____

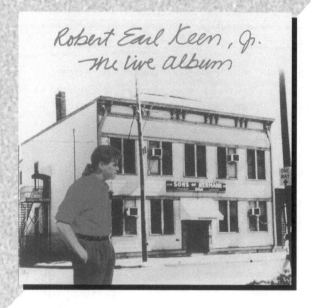

Robert Earl Keen, Jr.
The Live Album

SNUFF DIPPERS ALL... Bryan Duckworth, Robert, Dave Heath and Mark Patterson (all members of Robert's band). Photo taken during the Dallas/Fort Worth World Tour, December, 1993 at the Three Teardrops Saloon.

Robert attended Texas A&M University. He and his friend, Lyle Lovett, co-wrote <u>The Front Porch Song</u> about their view of life from the front porch of 302 Church Street, Robert's residence. Sunny Fitzsimons and Bryan Duckworth also lived at the house on Church Street. Here, Sunny and Robert practice Bluegrass tunes and are probably skipping class. Photo by Lyle Lovett

A steady hand and a determined gaze net 5-year-old Will Grote the thrill of victory at the pop gun booth. The young Bryan cowboy chose an American flag as his prize. Another cowboy having a good time whooping it up is Robert Keen of the Front Porch Boys.

Robert sings I Would Change My Life. Nanci Griffith recorded this song for her *Little Love Affairs* album.

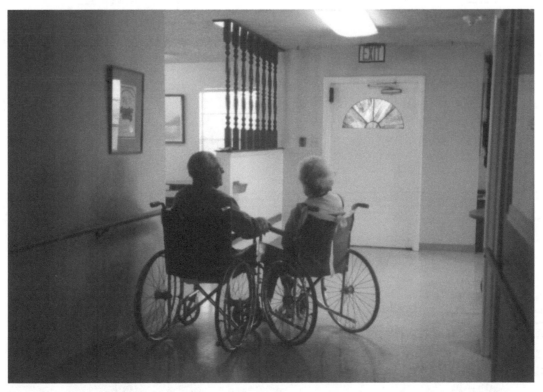

Robert and Fred Koller co-wrote I Wanna Know about their experiences with the aged and particularly Robert's friends in the Bandera Nursing Home.
Photo by Kathleen Keen

Copenhagen

Words and Music by
ROBERT EARL KEEN

wait - in' there _ be - tween my cheek and gum _____
swal - low and __ then threw her pop - corn up _____
ha - gen if ____ you wan - na snuff 'em out _____

CHORUS

Co - pen - ha - gen   what a wad ___ of fla - vor ___

Co - pen - ha - gen you can see it in ____ my smile ____

Co - pen - ha - gen   do your - self a fa - vor Chew

Co - pen - ha - gen Drive them pret - ty girls ____ wild

1.,2.   3.

(Instrumental)

Co - pen - ha - gen drive them pret - ty girls ____

wild _____

The Front Porch Song

Words and Music by ROBERT EARL KEEN
and LYLE LOVETT

G
A

Em
F#m

porch is just a weath - ered grey-haired sev-en-ty years_ of Tex - as He's
(5.) Braz - os still runs mud-dy like she's run all a-long___ There ain't
(6.) porch is just a long_____ time wait - in' and for-get - tin' and re -

C
D

D
E

do - in' all he can__ not to give in to the cit - y and he al -
nev - er been no cane to grind the cot - ton's all but gone_ And you know this
mem - ber - in' the com - in' back not cry - in' 'bout the leav - in' And re - mem -

G
A

Em
F#m

- ways takes the rent__ late so long__ as I run his cat - tle He
Chev - ro - let pick - up truck_ she was some-thing back in 'six - ty Now there
- ber - in' the fall - in' down and the laugh - ter of the curse of luck from all

C
D

D
E

1., 2.

picks me up__ at din-ner - time_ I lis - ten to him rat - tle He says the
ain't no-bod - y lis - ten to him 'cause they all think he's cra - zy This old
those sons - of - bitch-es who said we'd nev - er

3.

D.C. al Coda

get back up

CODA

Em
F#m

C
D

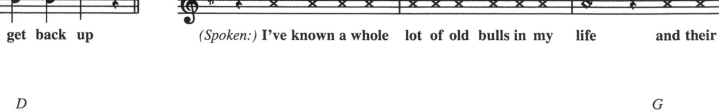

(Spoken:) I've known a whole lot of old bulls in my life and their

D
E

N.C.

G
A

work is nev - er done __

Goin' Down In Style

**Words and Music by
ROBERT EARL KEEN**

Fast (♩ = 116)

I left Hous-ton Tex-as in a gulf-coast hur-ri-cane ___ I was
I hit Cor-pus Chris-ti and the wind ___ was at my back ___ I

Instrumental

blown down by tor-na-does washed up by the rain ___ My
drove them wom-en cra-zy in my dad-dy's Cad-il-lac ___ I'd

Pap-py was-n't hap-py with ___ me he told me to go ___ I
cruise 'em up the bou-le-vard treat-ed 'em like queens ___ I

stole my dad-dy's Cad-il-lac ___ I head-ed down the road ___ I
took 'em all the pla-ces they want-ed to be seen ___ And

had a grin ___ from ear ___ to ear with each and ev-'ry mile ___ I'm
when I had ___ to leave ___ 'em I'd tell 'em with ___ a smile ___ I'm

I Wanna Know

Words and Music by ROBERT EARL KEEN
and FRED KOLLER

(1., 3.) Have you got a
(2.) Words can paint a

min - ute
pic - ture

a lit - tle time that we can spend
sharp - er than a pho - to - graph

O - pen up and let me in ___ share some mem - o - ries ___
I know you can take me back ___ to times I'll nev - er see ___

Peo - ple in a hur - ry ___ ev - 'ry day goes ___ by so fast
Got a lot of ques - tions ___ there's so much I ___ want to learn

No one takes the time to ask ___ how it used to be ___ I wan-na know
You can make the pag - es turn ___ you're liv-ing his - to - ry ___

CHORUS

did your fa - ther own an au - to - mo - bile or a two - horse car-riage with wood -

- spoke wheels ___ I hear you used to walk to school ___ sev-en miles a day ___

Did you ev - er ride a rail-road train And the ver - y first time you saw ___

___ a plane ___ did you think the world ___ had gone ___ in - sane ___ Tell me what you got to say ___

1.
I want to ___ know ___

2.

D.S. al Coda

know ___

CODA

share some mem - o - ries

I Would Change My Life

Words and Music by ROBERT EARL KEEN

Moderately (♩ = 80)

Guitar
(capo 4th fret): Dsus4
Keyboard: F#sus4

VERSE

nev - er liked this place__ where we've_ been liv - in' all__ a - long___ So
I have spent my hours__ on __ some mis - be - got - ten dreams__ And
wish that I could find__ the words. to make you come. back home__ I

you packed up __ your things_ and bought _ a one - way tick-et home __
I have spent _ my mon - ey on __ some fool - ish - heart - ed things __ And
wish that I __ could say __ the things_ you've need - ed for so long __ I

Leav - in' nev - er hurts_ as much __ as be - in' left __ be - hind _____
I have spent _ my mem - o - ries ___ on old and bit - ter wine _____
wish that you __ could see __ me now __ may - be then_ you'd find _____

CHORUS

I would change __ my life __ I would make _

To Coda
(third time)

__ it right _ I would change. my life __ if you would on — ly change _ your

Robert Earl Keen, 1979.
Photo by Pat Johnson

Robert Earl Keen, John Hiatt, Joe Ely, Guy Clark and Lyle Lovett on the Marlboro Tour. During this tour Joe heard REK's songs The <u>Road Goes On Forever</u> and <u>Whenever Kindness Fails.</u> Soon after Joe cut both songs for his *Love and Danger* album.

In 1994 Robert performed in the play "Chippy." Butch Hancock, Joe Ely, Wayne "The Train" Hancock and Jo Harvey and Terry Allen (author of *Amarillo Highway*) performed also. Jo Harvey and Terry Allen adapted the play from a West Texas' hooker's diaries. Here are members of the cast and friends on opening night in Philadelphia, PA.

Mariano Dominguez Luna
1988 Bandera, Texas

Robert, Kathleen and long-time friend and Austin, Texas promoter, Griff Luneburg. Griff has promoted shows at the Cactus Cafe and the Paramount Theater in Austin for many years.

It's The Little Things

Words and Music by
ROBERT EARL KEEN

Love's A Word I Never Throw Around

Words and Music by
ROBERT EARL KEEN

CHORUS

Love's a word __ I nev-er throw a-round __
So when I say I'll love __ you 'til the end __
I'm talk-in' 'bout __ un - til the day __ they
lay me in the ground __
Love's a word __ I
nev-er throw a-round _____

(2.)And I'd
(3.) So I'm

Additional Lyrics

3. So I'm going to the country spend some time out in the woods
Counting stars and sleeping all alone
And I can't say for certain it'll do me any good
But it's time I grew accustomed to being on my own

Chorus

Mariano

Am   F   G   C

**Words and Music by
ROBERT EARL KEEN**

Moderately fast (♩ = 90)

Guitar
(capo 2nd fret): Am
Keyboard: Bm

(1.) The man out - side he works _
(2.- 7.) *See additional lyrics*

_ for me _ His name _ is Mar - i - a - no He cuts _

_ and trims the grass _ for me _ he makes _ the flow - ers

bloom He says that he comes from a place _ not far from Gua - na - jua -

- to It's two days on a bus _ from here _ a life - time from this room _

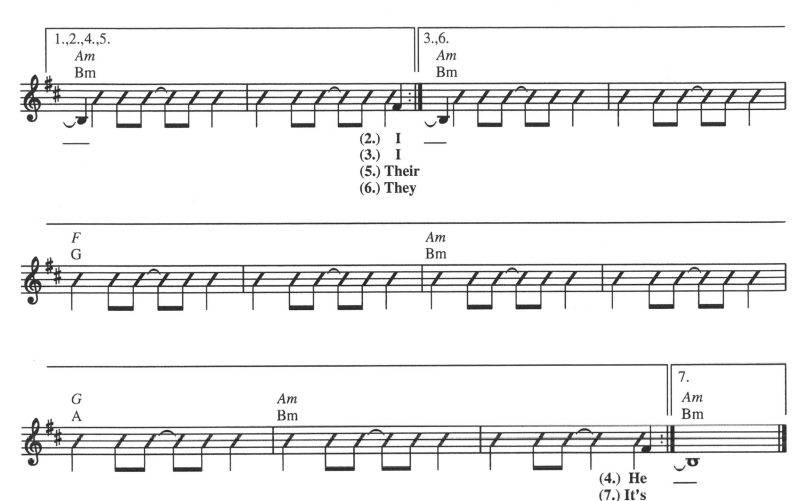

Additional Lyrics

2. I fix his meals and talk to him in my broken Spanish
   He points at things and tells me names of things I can't recall
   But sometimes I just can't but help from wondering who this man is
   And if when he is gone will he remember me at all

3. I watch him close he works just like a piston in an engine
   He only stops to take a drink and smoke a cigarette
   And when the day is ended I look outside my window
   There on the horizon Marino's silhouette

4. He sits upon the stone in a south-easterly direction
   I know my charts I know that he is thinking of his home
   I've never been the sort to say I'm into intuition
   But I swear I see the faces of the ones he calls his own

5. Their skin is brown as potter's clay their eyes void of expression
   Their hair is black as widows' dreams their dreams are all but gone
   They're ancient as the vision of the sacrificial virgin
   Innocent as crying from a baby being born

6. They hover 'round the dying flame and pray for his protection
   Their prayers are often answered by his letters in the mail
   He sends them colored figures he cuts from strips of paper
   And all his weekly wages saving nothing for himself

7. It's been a while since I have seen the face of Mariano
   The border guards they came one day and took him far away
   I hope that he is safe down there at home in Guanajuato
   I worry though I read there's revolution every day

The Road Goes On Forever

TUNING: D A D G B D (Low to High)

**Words and Music by
ROBERT EARL KEEN**

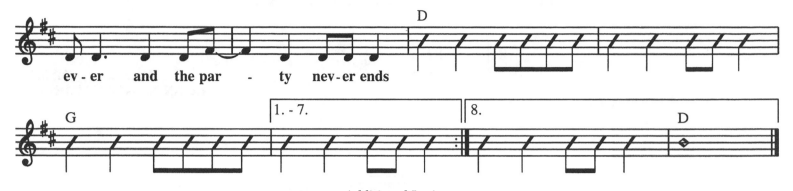

ev - er   and   the par - ty   nev - er ends

Additional Lyrics

2. Sonny was a loner older than the rest
   He was going in the Navy but couldn't pass the test
   So he hung around town he sold a little pot
   The law caught wind of Sonny and one day he got caught
   But he was back in business when they set him free again
   The road goes on forever and the party never ends

3. Sonny's playing eight ball at the joint where Sherry works
   When some drunken out-of-towner put his hands up Sherry's skirt
   Sonny took his pool cue laid the drunk out on the floor
   Stuffed a dollar in her tip jar and walked on out the door
   She was running right behind him reaching for his hand
   The road goes on forever and the party never ends

4. They jumped into his pickup Sonny jammed her down in gear
   Sonny looked at Sherry said "Let's get on out of here"
   The stars were high above them the moon was in the east
   The sun was setting on them when they reached Miami Beach
   They got a motel by the water and a quart of Bombay gin
   The road goes on forever and the party never ends

5. They soon ran out of money but Sonny knew a man
   Who new some Cuban refugees that dealt in contraband
   Sonny met the Cubans in a house just off the routes
   With a briefcase full of money and a pistol in his boot
   The cards were on the table when the law came busting in
   The road goes on forever and the party never ends

6. The Cubans grabbed the goodies Sonny grabbed the jack
   He broke the bathroom window and climbed on out the back
   Sherry drove the pickup through the alley on the side
   Where a lawman tackled Sonny and was reading him his rights
   She stepped out in the alley with a single-shot .410
   The road goes on forever and the party never ends

7. They left the lawman lying they made their getaway
   Got back to the motel just before the break of day
   Sonny gave her all the money and he blew a little kiss
   "If they ask you how this happened say I forced you into this"
   She watched him as the taillights disappeared around the bend
   The road goes on forever and the party never ends

8. It's Main Street after midnight just like it was before
   Twenty-one months later at the local grocery store
   Sherry buys a paper and a cold six-pack of beer
   The headlines read that Sonny is going to the chair
   She pulls back onto Main Street in her new Mercedes Benz
   The road goes on forever and the party never ends

Sonora's Death Row

**Words and Music by
KEVIN "BLACKIE" FARRELL**

1. Me and the boys __ we
(2.- 7.) *See additional lyrics*

cinched up our sad-dles and rode __ to So-no-ra last night __ Guns __

__ hang-in' proud and dar-in' out loud __ for an-y-one look-in' to fight __

__ Card __ cheats and rus-tlers would run __ for their holes __ when the boys __

__ from the old Bro-ken O __ rode up and reigned __ on the street __

__ that they named So-no-ra's Death __ Row

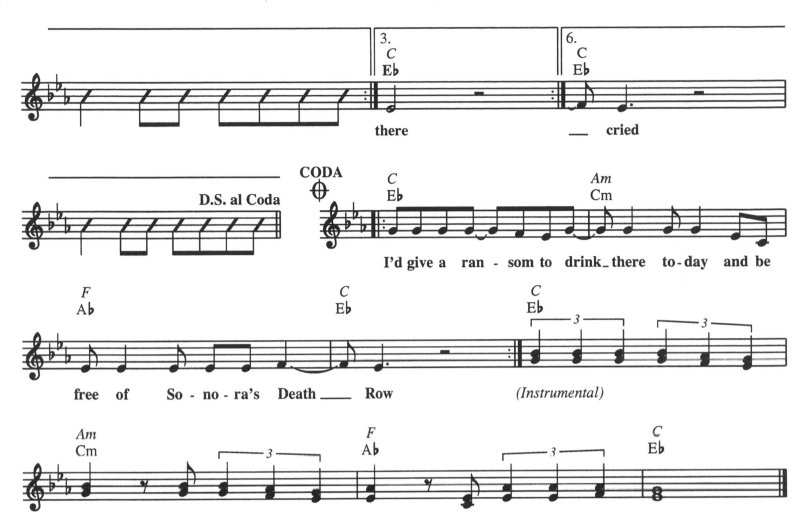

there ___ cried

CODA

D.S. al Coda

I'd give a ran-som to drink_ there to-day and be

free of So-no-ra's Death ___ Row   (Instrumental)

Additional Lyrics

2. Mescal is free in Amanda's Saloon for the boys from the old Broken O
   Saturday nights in the town of Sonora are best in all Mexico
   They got guitars and trumpets sweet señoritas who won't want to let you go
   You'd never believe such a gay happy time on a street called Sonora's Death Row

3. Inside Amanda's we was a-dancin' with all of Amanda's gals
   I won some silver at seven card stud so I was outdoin' my pals
   But the whiskey and mescal peso cigars drove me outside for some air
   Somebody whispered "Your life or your money" I reached but my gun wasn't there

4. *Instrumental*

5. I woke up face down in Amanda's back alley aware of the fool I had been
   Rushed to my pony grabbed my Winchester then entered Amanda's again
   Where I saw my partners twirlin' my pistols and throwin' my money around
   Blinded by anger I jacked the lever and one of them fell to the ground

6. Amanda's went silent like night in the desert my friends stared in pure disbelief
   Amanda was kneelin' beside the dead cowboy plainly expressing her grief
   And as I bowed my head a tremble shot through me my six gun was still at my side
   I felt my pockets there was my money I fell to my knees and I cried

7. A nightmare of mescal was all that it was for no one had robbed me at all
   I wish I was dreamin' the sound of the gallows they're testin' just outside the wall
   Mescal's still free in Amanda's Saloon for the boys from the old Broken O
   I'd give a ransom to drink there today and be free of Sonora's Death Row
   I'd give a ransom to drink there today and be free of Sonora's Death Row

Five Pound Bass

**Words and Music by
ROBERT EARL KEEN**

(1.) Up _____ this morn - ing _____ be - fore _____ the sun
(2.) Down by the lake - side _____ just off _____ the ramp
(3.-5.) *See additional lyrics*

fixed me some cof - fee and a hon - ey bun
all them peo - ple sleep - in' in their fish - in' camp

Jumped in my pick - up _____ gave her the gas _____ I'm
Some out in the pup _____ tents _____ some out in the grass _____ they

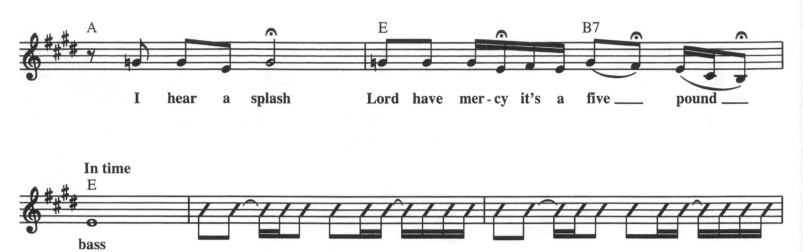

I hear a splash　　Lord have mer-cy it's a five___ pound___

In time

bass

(Spoken: That's a five pound bass son)

Additional Lyrics

3. Jump in my john boat I stow all my gear
   I fire her up and when I am in the clear
   I sail across that water as smooth as glass
   Ready here I come you five pound bass

4. I find the perfect spot some old dead trees
   Back in a canyon where you can't feel no breeze
   I tie my lure I make my cast
   It's breakfast time you five pound bass

5. That old sun is rising that water's clear
   I watch my lure as it's flying through the air
   I see a ripple I hear a splash
   Lord have mercy it's a five pound bass
   (That's a five pound bass son)

REK live performance.
Photo by Peter D. Figen

REK at Gruene Hall, Texas' oldest dance hall.
Photo by Peter D. Figen

Corpus Christi Bay

**Words and Music by
ROBERT EARL KEEN**

Guitar
(capo 3rd fret): G
Keyboard: B♭

Moderately (♩ = 120)

VERSE

I worked the rigs from three 'til mid - night _____ on the Cor - pus Chris - ti Bay _____

I'd get off and drink 'til day - light _____ sleep the morn - in' a - way _____

I had a plan to take my wa - ges, _____ leave the rigs _ be - hind for

good _____ But that life it is con - ta - gious _____ and it gets. down in your

blood _____ I lived in Cor - pus with my bro - ther _____
My bro - ther had a wife and fam - 'ly _____
Now my bro - ther lives in Hous - ton _____

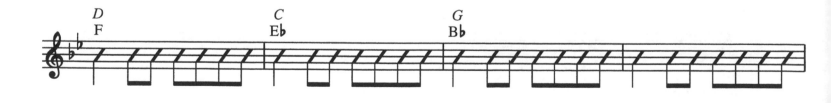

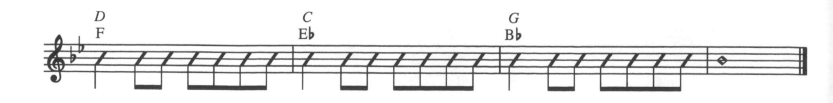

Jesse With The Long Hair Hangin' Down

Words and Music by
ROBERT EARL KEEN

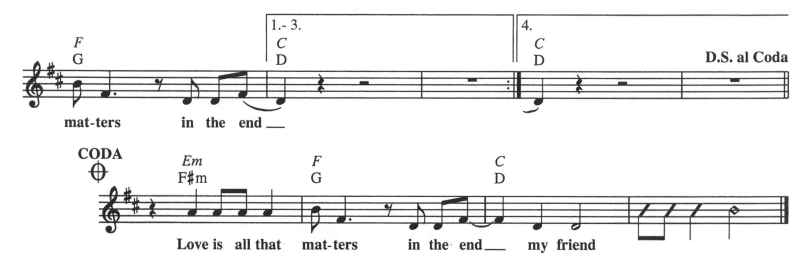

mat-ters   in the end ___

CODA

Love is all that mat-ters   in the end ___ my friend

Additional Lyrics

2. Sheriff Paul was sleepin' his hat off in his lap
When he got a package that woke him from his nap
He unrolled a poster couldn't help but frown
It was Jesse with the long hair hangin' down
They had been compadres many years before
Jesse saved his life one time back before the war
Now he was the king of thieves he wore it like a crown
Jesse with the long hair hangin' down

Chorus

3. Mr. Brown the banker hid the money in his case
It was time for him to leave this godforsaken place
His true love loved the outlaw who hated Mr. Brown
That was Jesse with the long hair hangin' down
Mr. Brown had taken the land that Jesse owned
The banker claimed that Jesse had not repaid his loan
Truth and lies were tangled but when the truth unwound
There was Jesse with the long hair hangin' down

Chorus (Instrumental)

4. Mr. Brown was all alone Luann came walking in
She pulled a pistol from her purse and pointed it at him
When the door blew open she turned to look around
It was Jesse with the long hair hangin' down
Mr. Brown grabbed Luann's gun and held it to her head
"I'll blow her to kingdom come" is what the banker said
In that fateful moment Jesse stood his ground
Jesse with the long hair hangin' down

Chorus

5. The bullet that killed Mr. Brown came through the windowpane
It put a hole above one eye and lodged down in his brain
He never saw a puff of smoke no flash no fire no sound
From Jesse with the long hair hangin' down
Sheriff Paul was fast asleep his hat down on his eyes
When he got a letter and much to his surprise
A picture of the sweet Luann in her wedding gown
And Jesse with the long hair hangin' down

Flesh and blood it turns to dust
Scatters in the wind
Love is all that matters in the end my friend

Whenever Kindness Fails

Words and Music by
ROBERT EARL KEEN

I crossed the des-ert on a din-ing car ___ in the spring of nine-ty-
The moon was in the sign of Scor-pi-o ___ the sun was at my
I on-ly have a mo-ment to ex-plain just a chance to let you

one ___ I met some peo-ple drink-ing at the bar ___
back ___ I did-n't know how far the train would go ___
know ___ When it's time for you to board the train ___

they were laugh-ing hav-ing fun ___ I told 'em that I had-n't
un-til the law would find my track ___ I saw the brake-man and the
there are two ways you can go ___ You can ride the wheels in -

heard the joke ___ that was so hi-lar-i-ous ___
en-gi-neer ___ drink-ing wine and eat-ing brie ___
to the sun ___ feel the wind up-on your face ___

They said that I was just a dumb cow-poke
I asked 'em who would brake and who would steer
Or you can laugh in-to a load-ed gun

I did-n't want to make a
they start-ed point-ing back at
and you'll like-ly lose your

CHORUS

fuss ___
me ___ }
place _ }

So I shot 'em down   one by   one ___   then I left 'em ___ 'long the rails ___

To Coda
(third time)

I use my gun ___ when-ev-er kind-ness fails ___

1.

2.

D.C. al Coda

CODA

fails _____   Yeah I   shot 'em down

one by   one ___   then I   left 'em ___   'long the   rails _____   When I

use my   gun _____   that lone-some   whis-tle   wails _____

47

Robert and Kathleen at Mi Tierra's Restaurant, San Antonio, Texas. Photo by fellow dinner guest and off-duty Austin City Limits official photographer, Scott Newton.

Merry Christmas from the family.
Photo by Paul S. Howell

Rich Brotherton, Mark Patterson, Bryan Duckworth and Robert share BBQ before a Luckenbach, Texas gig.
Photo by Peter Figen

Robert at home in Bandera, Texas, Cowboy Capital of the World, 1993.
Photo by Ralph Sauer

Barbeque

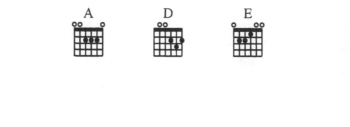

Words and Music by
ROBERT EARL KEEN

Moderately ($\bullet$ = 120)

A

(1.) Oh

VERSE

A

when I was a lit-tle boy on - ly one or two ___ the

(2.-5.) *See additional lyrics*

first thing I did en - joy ___ was a plate of bar - be - que ___

CHORUS

D

Bar - be - que ___ sliced beef and bread ___ ribs and sau-sage and a cold Big Red ___

A

Bar-be-que makes old ones feel ___ young Bar-be-que makes ev - 'ry-bod - y some-one ___

E

To Coda ⊕ D
(fifth time)

If you're feel-in' pu - ny and you don't know what to do ___ treat your - self to some meat

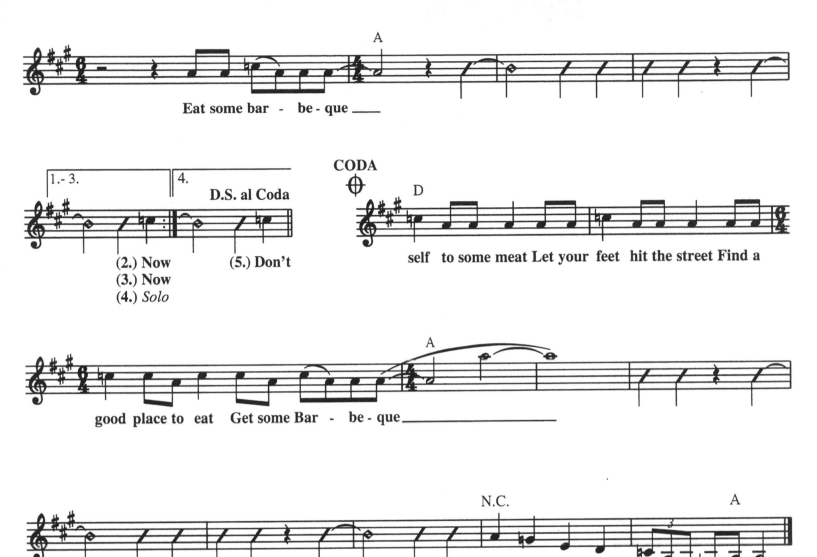

Eat some bar - be - que _____

(2.) Now   (5.) Don't
(3.) Now
(4.) Solo

self to some meat Let your feet hit the street Find a

good place to eat Get some Bar - be - que_____

Additional Lyrics

2. Now there was once this girl I knew
   She treated me so mean
   I offered her my Barbeque
   She licked my platter clean

   Chorus

3. Now don't give me no broccoli
   Or any Swiss fondue
   Baby if you want to rock me
   Give me good ole Barbeque

   Chorus

4. *Instrumental (Verse and Chorus)*

5. Don't send me to heaven it
   Ain't where I should go
   'Cause the devil's got a charcoal pit
   And a good fire down below

   Chorus **(To Coda)**

Gringo Honeymoon

**Words and Music by
ROBERT EARL KEEN**

Moderately (♩ = 96)

VERSE

(1.) We were stand-in' on ___ a moun-tain-top
(2.-5.) *See additional lyrics*

where the cac - tus flow-ers grow

I was wish-in' that the world ___ would stop

not in sight _ and we dreamed _ all af - ter - noon __

We asked _ the world _ to wait _ so we could

cel - e - brate _ a gring - o hon - ey - moon _

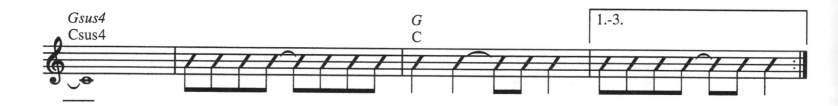

D.S. al Coda

CODA

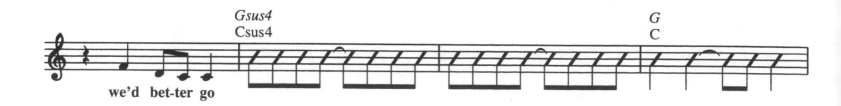

we'd bet-ter go

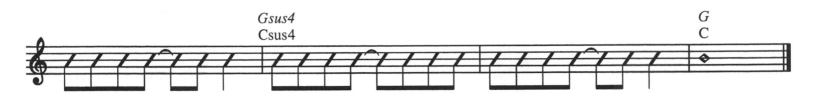

Additional Lyrics

2. We stepped out onto the golden sand
   The sun was high and burning down
   Rented donkeys from an old blind man
   Saddled up and rode to town
   Tied our donkeys to an ironwood tree
   By the street where the children play
   We walked in the first place we could see
   Servin' cold beer in the shade

   Chorus
   We were drinkin' like the end was not in sight
   And we drank all afternoon
   We asked the world to wait so we could celebrate
   A gringo honeymoon

3. Met a cowboy who said that he
   Was runnin' from the DEA
   He left a home a wife a family
   When he made his getaway
   We followed him on down a street of dust
   To his one-room rundown shack
   He blew a smoke ring and he smiled at us
   I ain't never goin' back

   Chorus
   We were flyin' like the end was not in sight
   And we soared that afternoon
   We asked the world to wait so we could celebrate
   A gringo honeymoon

4. He said there's one last place that you should go
   He took us to the town's best bar
   He knew a crusty caballero
   Who played an old gut-string guitar
   And he sang like Marty Robbins could
   Played like no one I've known
   For a while we knew that life was good
   It was ours to take back home

   Chorus
   We were singin' like the end was not in sight
   And we sang all afternoon
   We asked the world to wait so we could celebrate
   A gringo honeymoon

5. We were standin' on a mountaintop
   Where the cactus flowers grow
   I was wishin' that the world would stop
   When you said we better go

Merry Christmas From The Family

Words and Music by
ROBERT EARL KEEN

I'm Comin' Home

Words and Music by
ROBERT EARL KEEN

Packed my suit-case and I racked my brain __
They threw a par-ty there from dusk 'til dawn __ Seems like
I drove for-ev-er out to God knows where __

bought a tick-et on __ a late-night train __ Took a tax - i through the
ev-'ry-bod-y knows __ old sleep-y John __ He said next time I bet - ter
Come ten-thir-ty there __ was no one there __ They could-n't pay me but I

pour - in' rain _____ I'm com-in' home _ to you __
bring you a - long _____ I'm com-in' home _ to you __
did - n't care _____ I'm com-in' home _ to you __

CHORUS

Flew from Bos-ton out to San Jo - sé ___ Saw our old __ friends _ in
They had fresh caught sal-mon on the bar - be - ques _ There were peo-ple jam - min' to the
I'm feel - in' bet-ter since I got your card. I read it o - ver and o - ver when the

Mon-te - rey ___ Bay ___ When they asked me if I'd ___ like to stay _ I said I'm
all - night. blues _ Life is good out in ___ San - ta Cruz _ but I'm
road gets __ hard _ Ain't noth - in' bet - ter than your __ own back yard _ I'm

com-in' home _ to you ___ I'm _____
com-in' home _ to you ___
com-in' home _ to you ___

com-in' home _ Made up my mind that's what I'm _ gon-na do _ Can't love no-bod-y on the

tel - e - phone _____ I'm com-in' home _ to you ___

Think It Over One Time

E   F#m   A   C#m   B7   G#

Words and Music by
ROBERT EARL KEEN

Lively (♩ = 114)

(Instrumental)

VERSE

1. You say you're
(2.-4.) *See additional lyrics*

clear- in' out __ The dev-il's in __ your eyes   No time to walk __

__ no time to talk __ no time for long __ good - byes __

The tick- et's in __ your hand   You've made that fi - nal call __

the hard words fly-in' by __ like punch-es in a bar - room brawl ___

CHORUS

We've made a mess __ of things It makes _ no

dif-'rence now ___ Let's chalk it all ___ up to the blues ___

Lit - tle girl ___ think it o - ver one

time _ Lit - tle girl ___ think it o - ver one

time _ Lit - tle girl ___ think it o - ver one

1.-3.

time be - fore ___ you break

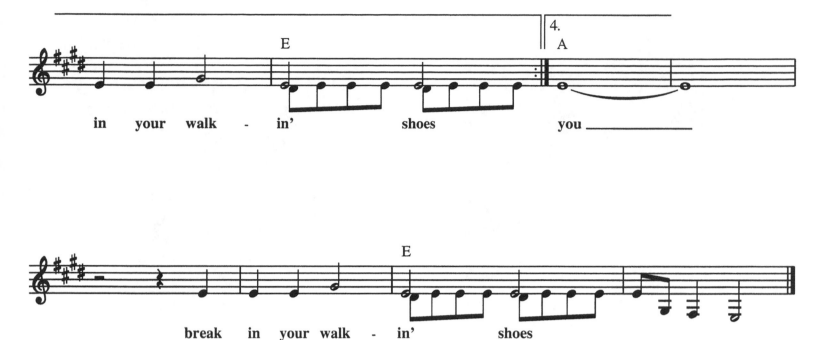

in   your   walk -   in'   shoes   you _____

break   in   your   walk - in'   shoes

(Instrumental)

Additional Lyrics

2. I am just what I am
   I won't apologize
   So if you go you'll surely know
   You'll have to come to realize
   Love don't walk away
   Only people do
   So if you go or if you stay
   You know I'll keep on lovin' you

   Chorus

3. We've made the hard times sing
   We've made the miles go by
   We've broken both our wings
   And still we've had the will to fly
   It ain't the memories
   That make me talk this way
   It's more like someone pulled the plug
   Before we ever saw the play

   Chorus

4. I've read a thousand books
   I've been behind the wheel
   I've known you all my life
   But still I can't feel how you feel
   It's only you for me
   Just like the whooping crane
   Who has one mate for all his life
   And if she dies he'll do the same

   Chorus

ROBERT EARL KEEN

DAVE HEATH

BRYAN DUCKWORTH

MARK THOMAS PATTERSON

Photos by Peter D. Figen

RICH BROTHERTON